NOTES TO MY SONS

This book is dedicated to my loving wife Renae.

She continues to be my biggest supporter and nurturer of my dreams.

Renae, I love you to life!

Acknowledgments:

Ruth Ramos Clifford-Editor

Katherine Evans-Editor

Dustin Claridy-Cover Art

CONTENT

FOREWARD

"ANOTHER FATHER'S VIEW"

PASTOR EDWIN MOORE has compiled a series of writings that could be compared to Apostolic Epistles of the First Century. Each discourse is filled with life, health and wisdom like unto Solomon's series of thoughts and advice to youth and the aged. Each letter or chapter is carefully crafted so as to give clear roadmaps to an intended destination.

When reading this volume, one enters the heart and mind of a true shepherd. The writings lack the sound of a man in resignation but the readings provide historical value and cameos into a leader's childhood, puberty, adulthood and approach to seniority.

My advice to the reader would be to, recreationally, read the text and then return to it for life-study. Reading Pastor Moore's script makes me wish I had penned more of my own experiences so that I could assist our young men and women in their journeys of life.

Finally, the text does not seek to postulate theology but one can find clear paths to Christ and His call to all mankind herein. You will appreciate the "commercial breaks" and the humor amidst the serious circumstances of life. Edwin and **Renae** have been parents to a couple dozen children during their sojourn and they, more than, qualify to be seen and heard. God bless their work and God bless all who will read and bless them.

† J. DELANO ELLIS **II**

METROPO LITAN-ARCHBISHOP

JOINT COLLEGE OF AFRICAN–AMERICAN BISHOPS

My wife, Renae, and I have been married for fifteen wonderful years. She is truly an amazing woman, wife, my best friend and mother to our children. We have been instrumental in parenting over a dozen children, most of them boys and at some point most of them living in our home at one time or another. There was never a dull moment in our home.

At this point in my life, I have come to grips with the thought that we will never have our own biological children. If I am totally honest, I would have to say that every once in a while the thought of having my own biological children crosses my mind. What would it be like to give birth to a child that has come from my loins? What would it be like to hold a newborn and day after day look into his or hers eyes and see their eyes and nose and smile begin to look like me? What would it be like to hold that infant against my bare chest and feel its heartbeat against mine and know that the blood that flows through its small body is my blood?

Again, being transparent I would not be telling the truth if I told you I was never sadden by our circumstance.

There are times when I have found myself angry at God. Here we are, a happy, loving, a spiritually strong couple who trust God for everything. We can minister to everyone else's situation and have seen God use us to do the miraculous in other people's lives. We have watched God do many things for us and others in the supernatural, but we can't accomplish the most natural act of child birth. I don't dwell on it much these days. I find joy in the children that God *has* given us and some of them are marrying and having biological children of their own. Perhaps grand parenting will be a subject for another time.

I believe that being a parent is one of God's most precious gifts. I fear that it is a fabric of our society that is slowly being unwoven by the multiple snares of life. Internet, unemployment, broken families, over worked parents and other social and economic problems have us so consumed and rallying to the next movement that we neglect our most precious asset of family. Along with this gift comes an awesome responsibility. It's a labor of love that is often thankless, filled with long hours and sometimes disappointment. Yet, with every scraped knee, every bed tucking and parent teacher meeting, with every doctor visit, every sports event, every graduation and the proverbial broken heart from that first love relationship, a parent seizes the moment to teach, nurture and love that child not because of any award or accolades but because they realize the value of the gift entrusted to them.

The idea for this book was sparked by a series of posts that I put up on Face Book and Twitter. I did this for over a month and began to receive many responses and words of thanks. One young man sent me an inbox message on Facebook and said, "I wish you would have started this six months ago. I might still be married." I knew then that I needed to share this on a larger platform and share it with the many young men who didn't have fathers who understood the value of their gifts. I felt I needed to help those young men who were left to fend for themselves without the proper guidance through manhood that only another man can provide.

As I began to reflect on my relationship with my sons in contrast to the relationship I had with my father, the late Eddie L. Moore, I realized some things about him and about myself. My father was an amazing man, not a perfect man, but I believe he tried to do the best he could with whatever image of manhood was painted in front of him. He never knew his biological father and to my knowledge was primarily raised by his grandmother in Alabama.

Growing up, I remember my father didn't say much. He suffered from the same genetic disposition of most men; the inability to verbally communicate openly and freely! Most of what I learned from my father in my youth was what *not* to do. He was an intelligent man but didn't always make the best decisions. He didn't understand the value of what he had in the way of his family until it was too late. My father's infidelities and consequent affair which led to the birth of a child took its toll on my parent's marriage.

Why didn't he see the value in what he had in his own family? Why was it necessary for him to pursue a passion outside of his home? It wasn't because he wasn't needed or wanted. Perhaps no man ever spoke into his life that family is valuable. If it wasn't important enough to his own father, whom he never met, perhaps in his mind, it wasn't that big of a deal!

My father was a strong man but I can't help but to think how much more of a DAD he would have been had he been mentored or fathered properly. I often say any man can make a baby and be the father but not all fathers are dads. I see "Daddy" as being a term of endearment or an intimate title that is earned by action. How many sons (and daughters) are left wounded and bleeding because they don't have a dad who will take the time to nurture and teach them? How many have wrestled with homosexuality or low self-esteem because there was no dad to affirm their masculinity? How many became teen fathers or died young because there was no dad to role model self-control?

The void of "Dad" in our homes has dramatically affected the authenticity of son-ship. What I mean is, our boys have no role model to pattern themselves after. There is no older male figure in the home from which our boys can learn from while transitioning from boyhood to manhood. Our sons are being given a diluted version if any example at all of a genuine father and son relationship. Instead of building stronger families and generations we are producing self-centered, immoral, material-driven babies trapped in adult bodies. According to a study performed by the National Center for Fathering (NFC), fatherlessness has become an epidemic. Some fathering advocates would say that almost every social ill faced by America's children is related to fatherlessness. The NFC cites, poverty, substance abuse, physical and emotional health, educational achievement, crime, sexual activity and teen pregnancy as symptoms of fatherlessness. If our society has any hope of resurrecting manhood and fatherhood, it must start with dialog.

When Jesus was called upon because of the ailing Lazarus in John 11, the people thought all hope was lost when Jesus didn't show up and Lazarus ultimately died. Jesus tells the disciples that the sickness was not unto death. Even after Lazarus had fallen asleep (died), Jesus tells the disciples that he was going to wake him. It's that hope that stirs my spirit and gives me faith that manhood can be resurrected and restored.

When Jesus shows up, he reminds the mourning people that he is the resurrection. We find in John 11:41, Jesus begins a short dialog with his Father in heaven. At the end of this dialog he calls out to Lazarus by name and says two words. It was that dialog and those two words that changed everything. Two words made the difference between life and death. Two words quickened something in the supernatural and brought hope to a hopeless condition. Two words brought life and healing. Two words ratified a situation and brought clarity to who Jesus was while affirming who's he was. "Come forth".

([43] And when he thus had spoken, he cried with a loud voice, Lazarus, come forth.)

It is a long road to manhood and today is a good day to start your journey. My desire is to use this platform to share from a father's heart some things I feel are valuable lessons. Perhaps the man that was your biological father or the man that represented fatherhood to you was unable to have this dialog. Perhaps you are a mother or a wife who is reading this book as a means to start a dialog or challenge a boy or man in your life. I pray these notes will bless and encourage every son.

The men of God must begin a dialog. We must begin crying out to our father in heaven. 2 Chronicles 7:14 gives us the formula to bring healing to our nation and I believe this formula is also applicable to the restoration of manhood. Now is the time to cry out to our God and speak life into our sons. Sons, come forth!

Note #1

You are a male by gender but a MAN by integrity

In humans, each cell normally contains 23 pairs of chromosomes for a total of 46. Twenty-two of these pairs, called autosomes, look the same in both males and females. The 23rd pair, the sex chromosomes, differs between males and females. Females have two copies of the X chromosome, while males have one X and one Y chromosome.

This fact for me speaks to how God created woman (Eve), by going inside of a man (Adam), to bring her on the scene. Perhaps it was that other part of man, that Y chromosome that God reached inside of man and used to complete His masterpiece called mankind. When God took that rib from Adam to create his help meet, He took from what he had already declared was good and made it better.

Consistent with that, it also speaks to the responsibility of the man to nurture, love and protect that which came from him. I fear men have gotten away from the reality of responsibility and our roles have become topsy-turvy while women struggle to handle tasks for which they were never created. Aside from the obvious chromosomal differences, there is much more to developing your manhood than X's and Y's.

Just because you are anatomically endowed with organs that make you of the male gender does not make you a man. I once preached a message entitled, "Will the real men stand up?" Manhood in our culture has been so minimized that it is no wonder why we struggle to define its modern day role. Over periods of time, our expectations of real manhood seem to have been diminished.

Although the days of the knight in shining armor are gone, do we also do away with the code of honor they stood for? Do we fall into this false sense of relativism that tries to convince us that everything is alright and morality and values are not absolute? How can we be defined if we don't have a standard which sets the bar and separates us from the ordinary?

By definition Webster's Dictionary states that integrity is the firm adherence to a code of especially moral or artistic values. It is the state of unimpaired condition; soundness. Integrity is the quality or condition of being whole or undivided; completeness. Son, be a man of integrity. Have a moral belief system. Be sound in your dealings. You will find that this quality will open doors for you because people will see your integrity and know they can trust you.

The lack of integrity seems to be taking its toll on our society. Every time you look at the news or read a paper it is filled with stories of scandal. From the White House to the Church house, we are seeing high profile people being exposed and lives destroyed. It is important that you guard your integrity. It is important that you watch the company that you keep. Always keep your word. If you say you are going to do something then do it.

There are experiences and opportunities in my life that were presented to me strictly because of my integrity. Likewise I have avoided some situations not only because of how people see me, but also because of how I see myself. My integrity is too valuable to risk on a one night stand. What you will find is that people are not so quick to bring foolishness to your front door when they know you are a man of integrity.

There are circles of people that I won't hang around because of the perception that birds of a feather flock together. Most often your associations define who you are. Knowing who you are outside of a group takes away the group's ability to put you in compromising positions which may give a poor definition of who you are.

There is an old saying, "All I have in this world is my word". Learn to guard your integrity. Once it has been compromised, it may never fully recover. You see what everyone else is doing to get by and get ahead. You are not like everyone else nor do you have to be. Learn to celebrate your individuality. Live life with high standards and challenge people to meet you on your level.

Doing what's right is not always what's comfortable. Doing what's right may never win you a popularity contest. Sadly it seems like more and more people are willing to risk their integrity without even giving it a second thought. Our correctional institutions are overflowing with those who, instead of giving it a second thought, threw caution to the wind and along with it went their integrity, character and freedom. That same inability to make the right choices have produced fathers who don't know how to be dads. Two of the most common areas in a man's life where his integrity is tested are how he makes his money and who he is in covenant with.

In your business dealings, remember that everything that glitters is not gold. When you are presented with opportunities take the time to calculate the cost. If indeed something can jeopardize your integrity or your freedom, walk away from it. Although there are always risks associated with business, you know right from wrong.

Always take the high road and do the right thing. Even when it seems like no one will be affected or no one else will know, those are the times when what you do is more important. It is one thing to do what is right when all eyes are on you or you know how many cameras are watching. It is totally different when you know that no one else is watching and you are all alone. What you do when you are all alone will determine the level of integrity you have.

Just recently I heard a story on the news where a young man saw a blind man drop a $20 bill while he was waiting in line at a fast food restaurant. A woman in the line saw the money fall and she picked it up. Not thinking anyone was watching her, she placed the money in her purse. The young man saw the woman put the money in her purse and, realizing she had no plan to return the lost money to the rightful owner, he decided to confront her. The woman denied her actions and after exchanging a few words with the young man who worked at the restaurant she left without ordering anything herself.

The young man could have chosen to do nothing. He could have chosen not to get involved at all. He knew that for him to do nothing was wrong. Although the woman was not honest, he did the right thing by challenging her and calling her out. His actions up to that point demonstrated his integrity. He took a stand for what was right and even got involved. The actions he took after the confrontation were not surprising to me at all. The news reporter stated that the young man told the blind gentleman what had just happened and on behalf of the restaurant gave him $20.

The money that the young worker gave the blind gentleman didn't come from the restaurant; it came out of his own pocket. Someone that was in the restaurant at the time of the incident wrote a letter to the corporate office of the restaurant. The writer of the letter stated how impressed they were with the young man's service and integrity. The letter made its way to social media and the story went viral.

The young man has received calls, emails, interviews and offers including a phone call from one of the richest men in the world. The choice to do the right thing has opened doors and opportunities that were not present at the start of his shift that day. Being a man of integrity in your business dealings may not always have an immediate return, but you never know who is paying attention to your work and work ethic.

Some time ago, my wife and I did a series on covenant relationship. In a covenant relationship there is a deeper connection than just your casual interaction. In a covenant relationship, the expectations are more significant. The risks are greater and the value each person has for the other is considerable.

When you are in covenant with the right people, they push you to do better, be better and expect better. Those are the type of people you want on your side. People who will challenge you to be the best you can be. The sooner you identify those types of people and make those kinds of connections, the stronger you will be in every aspect of your life.

Chapter 1 questions

1. What does integrity mean to you?

_____

_____

_____

_____

_____

2. Why is integrity important?

_____

_____

_____

_____

_____

_____

_____

3. What person(s) from the Bible sticks out to you as someone with consistent integrity?

_____

_____

_____

_____

_____

_____

4. What actions do you need to take to raise the level of your integrity?

_____

_____

_____

_____

_____

_____

_____.

5. What men in your personal life or surrounding role model integrity?

_____

_____

_____

_____

Note #2

<u>When you become a man you must put away childish things. Real men master self-control and refrain from erratic emotional outburst.</u>

Son, this note has Biblical principle attached to it. You will find in 1Cor.13:11 the Bible says, "When I was a child, I spake as a child, I understood as a child, I thought as a child: but when I became a man, I put away childish things." As you are growing into manhood, I pray I am teaching you how to see things with a Godly man's perspective. You need to understand that how you see things at 16 should be different than how you see them at 26 and 36 and 46. Maturing chronologically but remaining a 16-year-old mentally, socially and spiritually is detrimental.

I have seen too many young men who have dropped out of school and have the appearance of being a Life Dropout. I will never understand how a 20-something year old could ever be comfortable living in his parents' or baby momma's house with no education, no job and playing video games the majority of the day. The children in the 80's TV commercial were speaking prophetically when they said "Silly rabbit, tricks are for kids."

What you were doing as an adolescent in many instances is no longer acceptable when you cross over into adulthood. There are new expectations and realities to explore and conquer. The way for you to be successful in this transition into manhood is for you to put those childish habits, mindsets and behaviors away. I'm not saying bury them, because some of those things will come in handy when you start a family and begin having children of your own.

Have you ever watched a grown man throw a temper tantrum? It is not a good look. Perhaps the image which I have painted in your mind is that of an adult man rolling around on the floor or stomping the floor and pouting. I think we can agree that any of these behaviors are inappropriate and childish.

Unfortunately, many men who have not mastered self-control revert back to childish behaviors. Maybe they don't fall out in the middle of a store or stomp away pouting but they display the equivalent of the child who is out of control. He can't verbalize how he really feels and lashes out towards his wife and family. He is physically and or verbally and emotionally abusive. Man out of control. This is the man who takes his pay check and instead of saving money or investing, he blows it on women, liquor, video games or whatever vice he uses to subdue and gratify his child like mindset. He is out of control. This is the man who won't keep a job and can always find fault with the employer. He legitimizes his failures and when challenged, he lashes out. Man out of control.

Growing up, I was spoiled. I didn't ask for much but when I asked for something it was usually a big ticket item. My parents always came through. Whether it was the full sized pin ball machine I got for Christmas or the Roland Juno-106 I got for my birthday, which was over $1000.00, they always gave me what I asked. I really had the illusion that I could have whatever I wanted whenever I wanted it. I was the only boy, the oldest and proud to say a "Momma's Boy". Like I said, I got whatever I wanted!

Those who really know me would argue that my philosophy relative to me thinking I could have whatever I want has not changed much. I never said I was perfect! Part of that belief is connected to my religious convictions. The God I serve is able to do exceeding abundantly above all I can ask or think according to Ephesians 3:20.

What has changed with my belief is that, while I believe I can have the desires of my heart, sometimes I have to wait. I have come to understand that sometimes I can't handle everything I want when I want it. I trust God to know what is best for me.

When I was in high school, I had a dream of being the next big R&B singer. Looking back at it now, I understand why God didn't allow it to happen. I don't think I would have handled that lifestyle well. Better yet, I think it would have taken me so far away from God and my true destiny that I would not have been able to recover.

Having self-control will afford you the ability to think things through. Life happens fast and you must pay attention and be a man of rational thought. Being in control of your emotions and not being the ticking time bomb that people are afraid to approach will add strength to your character and give people around you a sense of stability and safety.

The most common emotion that men display is that of anger or rage. Surely we are deeper than that! God created us in His image. The Bible does not limit the characteristics of God's nature to wrath. He is seen as a loving father, concerned parent, provider and more. Develop an emotional balance.

It is a powerful thing to see a man be secure and balanced enough in his emotions to be able to express his love to his son. It is even more powerful when that father can handle the responsibility of comforting his child during a loss or tragedy. We are not designed to be a hollowed shell when it comes to our emotions.

As you get older, you will need to assess what is and what isn't important. Some things or people who were relevant at one point in your life may not hold the same place down the road. There is nothing wrong with you when you realize that your circle of influence is changing.

It's a sign of you growing and maturing. Change, although painful at times, is necessary in this process.

A newborn baby has certain needs. It can't feed itself. It can't clothe or wash itself. Newborns have a certain diet. You wouldn't feed an infant prime rib with a loaded baked potato and a side of asparagus. It would be more than the child could handle. He wouldn't have the teeth to chew or the ability to properly digest that type of solid food. Likewise, you wouldn't call your teenager to the dinner table and have a bottle of milk and a bib waiting. Put away those things that at one point in your youth may have served you but as a man are now hindrances and distractions. Be mature enough to know when you've outgrown something. I see greater in you and this is not the time for distractions.

Chapter 2 questions

1. How was manhood celebrated in your home as a child?

_____

_____

_____

_____

_____

_____

_____

_____

2. Who taught you about manhood?

_____

_____

_____

_____

_____

_____

_____

3. What habits of your youth are distracting your growth spiritually?

_____

_____

_____

_____

_____

_____

_____

_____

4. What do you do when you get angry? Is it controlled or are you out of control and how do you know?

_____

_____

_____

_____

_____

_____

5. What areas of your life do you need to improve relative to self-control (i.e., money, sex, eating, emotional)?

_____

_____

_____

_____

_____

_____

_____

_____

_____

6. Identify possible solutions for the areas you need to improve.

_____

_____

_____

_____

_____

_____

_____ -

_____

_____

Note #3

Never be afraid to admit when you are wrong. Just don't make a habit of it!

My youngest son is so unlike the rest of our children. He can't seem to grasp the innate fact that I am always right. It doesn't matter what I say, he attempts to find some flaw or inaccuracy in my statement thus proving me wrong and therefore making him the smartest 15-year-old in history. He hates being wrong more than anything. We lovingly call him Google because of how he spends time looking up a lot of quirky little facts about everything. Jokingly around our house if someone needs to know something we say; "ask Google" and we all look at him.

One of the many colorful saying that my father had was, "If I don't know it, it ain't worth knowing". My father had a ton of one liners in his arsenal. Some made more sense than others. I will confess, the need to be right all the time is one of those things that I picked up from him. Was he always right? Of course not. No one is always right.

I remember one of the few times my father and I actually had a conversation while my parents were still married. He had the audacity to ask me why I thought he and my mother were getting a divorce. I decided to play his game and I recall saying something like "I have no idea. Why do you think Mom wants a divorce?" I think he pretended in the conversation to be oblivious to the reason himself. I assume this gave him some type of justification. I imagine that it allowed him to think that he was indeed a good husband and father in his own mind.

I'm not trying to demonize my father in this book. Overall, he was a good man. He was a great provider. We never really wanted for anything. He believed in working hard and taking care of his responsibilities. He was not a monster, just a man with some flaws. There were some wrinkles in his armor and the older he got, I think he could see more clearly how he had done some things wrong.

I imagine after the anointing left King Saul in 1 Samuel chapter 15 that he must have realized something was wrong. He must have realized that everything was wrong. Yet, instead of repenting and turning back to the

Lord, he continued in his transgression. He grew angry and jealous of young David. Instead of being a role model for David, Saul tried to kill him because he himself was wrong.

Today many sons are murdered mentally, spiritually and emotionally because their modern day Saul can't come to grips with his own shortcomings and imperfections. When you are in the wrong, the worst thing you can do is put on the façade that you are right and have it all together. You may be able to get over on some people with that act but eventually, the act gets old! People start to see right through you and your reputation and character are scarred.

Over the years after my parents divorced, my father and I developed a healthy relationship. We started meeting for lunch from time to time and having great discussions. Discussions about everything and nothing. I believe it was during one of those exchanges that he did it. My father admitted that he had done wrong by our family. He admitted it was the biggest mistake of his life. Being involved in extramarital affairs is what destroyed the best thing that ever happened to him and if he could take it back, he would.

It was that conversation that started me on the road to healing. I absolutely hated my father at one point in my life. His apology to me lifted a burden off of me that I had carried most of my life. His admitting that he was wrong taught me a valuable lesson in manhood that I will never forget. Being vulnerable didn't diminish my father's manhood to me. It actually fortified that he was man enough to admit he was wrong and capable of owning the hurt he caused my family.

Recently I had a similar moment with my son Anthony. I know I had disappointed him and there was no sense in trying to cover up, justify or minimize the issue. At that moment, I could have thrown up a wall. I could have been defensive or even downplayed how I hurt him.

No child wants to believe that underneath the cape, their superman is simply a man. Behind the smoke and mirrors, Dad is a man who is not perfect and is capable of making mistakes and being wrong. I think that being able to admit you are wrong shows how strong and secure you are.

Taking ownership for your actions is clearly one of the key elements missing in our society today. It's as if we con ourselves into thinking that even when we are wrong we are right and how dare anyone challenge what we believe! This is the mindset that has taken us to this place of relativism where it is only right or wrong based on how I feel and what works for me. If you subscribe to that point of view, then the level plain of morality becomes an unbalanced slippery slope void of consistency and value.

Before I do, say, plan or commit to things, I take the time to calculate the cost. I take into account what the ramifications will be if I say or do that. Do I have enough information to make that call, to have that opinion or take that action? Shooting straight from the hip may not always land the shot where it needs to go.

Chapter 3 questions

1. Identify an incident where you knew the prominent male figure in your life was wrong.

_____

_____

_____

_____

_____

_____

2. How did that person handle being wrong?

_____

_____

_____

_____

_____

_____

_____

3. What did you learn from their example?

_____

_____

_____

_____

_____

_____

4. When you are wrong do you make excuses or do you take responsibility and why?

_____

_____

_____

_____

_____

_____

_____

_____

5. Why is taking ownership for your actions important?

_____

_____

_____

_____

_____

_____

_____

_____

6. Can you think of anyone you need to apologize to because you were wrong? Who? Are you strong enough to do it?

_____

_____

_____

_____

_____

_____

_____

Note#4

Even the sower had to buy the seed before he could sow. Invest wisely into your harvest.

The concept of reaping and sowing has Biblical roots. The general idea behind "you reap what you sow" is that actions will have consequences. The effects of a person's behaviors are not necessarily apparent right away, such as when a farmer has to wait a while for a crop to mature. Nevertheless, it will show up eventually.

It's important that we always know where we are in life. The decisions you make today will affect you tomorrow. The question is how will they affect you? How will not paying attention in class today affect your ability to get into the college you want tomorrow? How will not going to college affect your ability to provide for yourself or your family? How will who you decide to have sex with affect your mental, physical and spiritual health? These and others are important questions you must ask yourself before you begin investing time, energy and resources.

Time is perhaps the most valued yet unappreciated commodity. Once it is spent, you cannot get it back nor can you exchange it. Often times, you might wish you could go back in time and handle something differently. You wish you could have responded differently or planned differently. The fact is, with every passing moment, you are sowing into your future. If you have a lot of dead time on your hands, don't expect to reap a full harvest.

There are so many things that you must take into consideration as it relates to your harvest. Just to clear things up for you, what I mean by your harvest is your future. Not only must you plant, nurture and protect the seed, you must also be mindful of where you get the seed from in the first place.

Some might argue that they are limited to the seed they have been given because of genetics or biological DNA. Some might dispute their ability to develop into anything beyond the characteristics of their mother and father. You may have her eyes and his nose. Your smile or your features may carry strong similarities but you don't have to produce from unrefined seed. You don't have to produce from the seeds of drug addiction, lying and sexual immorality. You don't have to produce from seeds of depression, rage or low self-esteem.

I am a firm believer in the greater factor that John spoke about in 1John 4:4. Stop allowing what you have been through and where you might have come from, limit where you are going. The reality is that if we all told our story, most of us have had to endure hard times at some point in our lives. If you have not experienced any trials in your lifetime, you are among a limited few. I challenge you to keep living.

1John 4:4(kjv) Ye are of God, little children, and have overcome them: because **greater** is he that is in you, than he that is in the world.

It is important to learn from life's obstacles. Find something that will make you a better person in every situation. It's easy to complain about the seeds you have been given to sow. It's easy to find fault with everyone around you who was supposed to nurture and cultivate you. It's easy to slip into a less than mindset and become content with a <u>have not</u> future. Don't play the blame game. Find something you can build off of - even if what you learned is what **not** to do.

One of the things my sons will tell you I love to do is go camping. If I had to survive in the wilderness, I think I would be alright. The serenity of sitting by a camp fire at night under the heavens and watching the concert of stars' shimmer in harmony is one of Gods greatest gifts. Not all of my sons see it the same way, but I think all of them will say they have been able to leave the camping trip with just a little more wisdom than what they had before the trip.

One of the things I enjoy doing while camping is being the first to get up in the morning. I like to get up early, sometimes even before the sunrise. The stillness of it all is so awesome to me. During this time, I often pray. I make my way over to where there was once a roaring fire. Although the fire is gone, I begin stirring in the ashes. Soon I find several embers. They are not producing enough heat to have a flame coming from them, but working together, the fire can live again.

By stirring and blowing and adding small amounts of kindling, the fire that was extinguished is now reignited. The fire on the inside of you is never totally gone. Life brings us situations that may try to overwhelm us. Even with all of your planning and all of your abilities, life happens. Before you know it, something has come and all but knocked the life out of you but you can recover.

Realize what you do today will affect your tomorrow. The decisions you make right now will shape your future. Reignite the flame and go back to school. Reignite the flame and take another shot at starting that business. It's not too late for a career change. It's not too late to start planning and saving.

Chapter 4 questions

1. Where do you see yourself in life right now?

    _____

    _____

    _____

    _____

    _____

    _____

2. What decisions have you made in the past that have
    had negative consequences later in life?

    _____

    _____

    _____

    _____

    _____

    _____

    _____

3. How could you have managed that situation differently?

_____

_____

_____

_____

_____

_____

_____

4. Why is time valuable?

_____

_____

_____

_____

_____

5. What fire needs to be reignited in you?

_____

_____

_____

_____

_____

_____

_____

_____

6. List possible resources you could seek out to ensure a rich harvest.

_____

_____

_____

_____

_____

_____

Note #5

<u>Please don't say "I do" if you really don't.</u>

This may be one of the most important notes I write to you. This note really embraces so many of the attributes of manhood that I hope to convey in this book. My wife and I always try to role model what a good working marriage looks like. We have always been open and transparent in front of people who look to us for guidance. I hope we have shown people what real love looks like. In our example of love, I hope people have seen our commitment to each other. I hope they have seen how we laugh, cry, struggle, overcome, disagree, communicate, and raised our family. Those are just some of the things associated with a healthy marriage.

Marriage is work! A successful marriage is always a work in progress. You have to be willing to "DO" the work involved with the "I DO's" you commit to at the wedding alter. How will you know if you are ready? How will you know if she is the "RIGHT" one? How will you know if this is who God has for you? Let me help you.

Often men are enamored with the idea of marriage or afraid to death of the commitment. I listen to young men talk about how they can't wait to be married and how it seems that everyone around them is either getting engaged or getting married. Eventually, coming home to an empty house gets old for most people and the realization sets in that God was on to something when He said it's not good for man to be alone.

I'm a firm believer that anything worth having is worth waiting for. Don't rush the process. Building anything requires a process. There are steps that need to be taken in building a relationship. It's not a race. Some people walk faster than others so don't gauge where you are based on where you see your family or friends.

The first thing I need to tell you before you even consider looking for a wife is start by getting you together. You can't relate to anyone if you haven't learned how to have a healthy relationship with yourself. Being the best you that you can be will make you feel better about yourself and make you more attractive to a woman who has ambition, goals and dreams. The saying is "Beauty is only skin deep", have something in your brain (education) and in your pocket (money) before you try to put a ring on her finger.

Have some life experience. I have seen young men who have never lived on their own struggle after they get married because they don't have experience doing basic things like: turning on utilities, paying utilities, clean, cook, balance a check book and other practical things a man should know how to do. You can't assume that the woman you will marry will know how to do any or all of these things. The key is you both will have strengths and weaknesses. Have those types of important discussions before you get married and plan how you will manage those responsibilities. If you have never had any experience, you don't bring much to the table.

Talk to some married people who have some longevity and a successful track record at being married. Although my parents divorced and my wife's parents were never married, we both feel we had good role models in our Pastors. Bishop John Hilton and Lady Shirley Hilton were my wife's examples and I learned from Pastor Harold W.

Luter and Lady Naomi Ruth Luter. These two couples were great teachers when it came to marriage. They lived what they were teaching. The Hiltons did our pre-marital counseling. To this day, I use Bishop Hilton's opening line when we counsel couples looking to be married. He started by asking the question, "What is your idea of the perfect marriage?"

If there was ever such a thing as the perfect marriage, I would argue that it was my Pastor and his wife. I never witnessed anything but the love which was radiant coming from the late Pastor Harold W. Luter and the late Lady Naomi Ruth Luter. I observed how he looked at her, how he held and affectionately kissed her in public. The way he would talk to her and how she would respond to each flirt and gesture. He was always a perfect gentleman relative to how he cared for her.

I recall traveling to Chicago with him for the last time on an annual fellowship trip with the church. Sis. Luter was not able to go because of health issues. As we got ready to check into the hotel room, I think it overwhelmed him as he called her to let her know that we had arrived safely. When he hung up the phone, he cried for a moment because she was not there at his side. If I had any doubt before with reference to whether what I had seen in their marriage over the 30 some years I had known them was real, that moment would have erased all doubt.

Pray and ask God for exactly what you want in a wife. There were certain qualities in a woman that I sought after. Of course, like any other man, beauty was a factor but more important was her relationship with God. I was already doing ministry and my wife would need to be compatible with me relative to doing ministry work. I didn't want a stay at home ministers wife or first lady. I wanted a woman who would enjoy doing ministry with me side by side. I wanted a strong Black woman who was an independent thinker yet knew how to love, respect and follow her husband. The Lord gave me that and so much more. Pray for what you want and be patient while you wait.

If done correctly, marriage will be one of the greatest things you will ever do in life. There will be ups and downs, ins and outs, tears and laughter, disagreements and reconciliations. Those are just some of the things you deal with between each other; I haven't mentioned all of the outside distractions and interferences you will have to contend with.

At times, this marriage journey can be like a roller coaster ride. Remember, I told you it is hard work. It takes more than a notion to be and stay married. The wedding vows are sacred and if you are going to be a man of integrity you will do whatever it takes to honor, protect and live out those vows. When you are in covenant with the woman that God has for you, it's easy to look into her eyes and know that it's you and her against the world. My wife and I see our marriage as an adventure and with each new day come new possibilities to explore. When you say "I do", mean it and keep your word.

2 Corinthians 6:14 (esv) Do not be unequally yoked with unbelievers. For what partnership has righteousness with lawlessness? Or what fellowship has light with darkness?

Chapter 5 questions

1. Do you plan on getting married? Why or why not?

_____

_____

_____

_____

_____

_____

2. Describe your role models relative to marriage and family.

_____

_____

_____

_____

_____

_____

_____

_____

3. What are you looking for in a wife? (This is what you should be praying for.)

_____

_____

_____

_____

_____

_____

4. What do you need to do in order to be prepared for marriage?

_____

_____

_____

_____

_____

_____

_____

5. How do you feel about divorce?

_____

_____

_____

_____

_____

_____

_____

6. There are 4 points I underlined in this chapter. Why do you think each is significant?

_____

_____

_____

_____

_____

_____

_____

_____

_____

Note #6

Actions speak louder than words

Son, there is an old saying; "Talk is cheap". Don't waste a lot of time trying to convince people about who you are- show them. Often times, people will try to sell you on or convince you that they are one thing or another. They might try to throw names or make claims about who they know or places they have been. It has been my experiences that people are who they will be. What a person does will most frequently reveal who they really are.

You will run across people who seem to be mixed with chameleon because they change in order to fit in. If the group is into one thing this month, then so are they. If the group is into something else next month, then so are they. Regardless of if they like it or not or agree with it or not, they will move with the group. At times, this will be due to them being clueless to who they are. At times, it will be in order to advance or gain favor with the group.

Proverbs 23:7(kjv) For as he thinketh in his heart, so is he…

Be able to stand on your own two feet. Have an opinion of your own. Be an independent thinker and don't spend too much time talking about who you are and where you're going. I say that for two reasons. First, everyone can't handle where you are going. Not only will they not support who you are, they may attempt to discourage you from reaching your full potential. Perhaps they think your goals and dreams are too wide and too extreme. They may try to convince you to downsize a little bit to fit their level of thinking. If you look into the mirror and see the CEO of a Fortune 500 company, strive to be that. Stop talking about it to people who only see you as a shift supervisor at a fast food restaurant.

Secondly, when you announce who you are becoming or who you have become, some around you will be envious. In the Old Testament Bible, Joseph was hated by his own brothers because he shared his dream. Because of his dream, they plotted against him. Because of his dream, he found himself entrapped in a pit. It was his dream which caused those who were supposed to love him and look out for him to conspire to kill him. They ultimately sold him into slavery all because of his dream.

People who are jealous are dangerous and capable of murder. It may not be the act of a physical murder they commit, but with every opportunity they will try to assassinate your name, slaughter your image or crucify your character. Talking to the wrong people will set you up for disappointment and disaster. Although you may have to go through your own pit experience, there is a palace on the other side of your pit.

A false sense of manhood is often grafted on young boys who have grown up with single mothers. These boys are often times told, "You are the man of the house". This frame of mind is not fruitful for a number of reasons. They can't be men and boys at the same time. Physically, mentally, emotionally, spiritually they are simply not equipped to handle the responsibilities of manhood at 5,11,13,16 and even beyond for some.

What examples of manhood has the child seen? Where is his father? Did his father abuse or demean his mother in front of him and now his view of manhood is to be explosive in relationships with females including his own mother? Did he witness his father commit crimes and now thinks that manhood is associated with thugging and robbing? When he was told "You are the man of the house now", based on his example, what did that mean to him? Was that then an excuse to walk away from responsibilities when things got a little tough?

This false sense of manhood has set the stage for many boys to grow up with a poorly conceived notion of what manhood is really about. They were made to believe they were "THE MAN" but in actuality they were still children, incapable of being a child and a man at the same time. Adults have the burden to care for the needs of children. Whatever the situation is, there is an adult who is charged with the responsibility of caring for the child.

Before a child comes into maturity, he will not understand the scope of what it takes to care for and meet his needs. Yet, in his mind he has been a man the whole time. Now what we have are a lot of adult males who suffer from the "Immagrownassman-syndrome". People with this condition often regularly publicize it. They are very adamant about letting you know they have it. Be sure you understand the more a person says or proudly announces "Immagrownassman", it's almost certain there is a scared little boy on the inside of him that is confused because they can't understand why you don't see it! Why can't you recognize they are a man? They have been told they were a man for years. The fact they are now actually of chronological age to be considered men, yet continue to act like and do boyish things and not get the same results confuses them and the response is usually to lash out in anger or run.

Celebrate your manhood. Be proud to be a man. Recognize that the banner of manhood can be quite heavy. When you actually carry the banner, you don't have to talk about it. People will know who you are and what you are about by your actions. Don't talk about being great. Be great! Don't talk about being successful. Be successful! Don't talk about starting the business. Start the business!

There have been potentially great men who have often missed out on their season because they have failed to act. Stop sitting around waiting for something to happen, make it happen. If you are paralyzed with fear or too lazy to take action in your life, you are not prepared for the challenge of manhood. You can't advance nor can you win if you're not even willing to get into the game.

Chapter 6 questions

1. What does the phrase "Actions speak louder than words." mean to you?

_____

_____

_____

_____

_____

_____

_____

2. List 5 accomplishments in your life as a result of you being a man of action.

_____

_____

_____

_____

_____

_____

_____

_____

3. List 5 goals that will not get accomplished in your life if you don't take action.

_____

_____

_____

_____

_____ -

_____

_____

4. What are your short and long term goals for the next 12 months?

_____

_____

_____

_____

_____

_____

_____

5. How is a false sense of manhood developed?

_____

_____

_____

_____

_____

_____

_____

6. What are some of the identifying characteristics of a male who may have a false sense of manhood?

_____

_____

_____

_____

_____

_____

_____

_____

Note# 7

Always Pray

When I was growing up, I clearly recall being in church on Sunday and listening to the old deacons of the church pray. As a young child, I have to admit, most of the time I didn't know what they were saying or what they were talking about. As I got older, the prayers and songs began to make a little more sense.

Luke 18:1(msg) Jesus told them a story showing that it was necessary for them to pray consistently and never quit.

It has been said that prayer is an essential staple in the life of any believer. There is an old church saying, "Much prayer, much power. Little prayer, little power. No prayer, no power." At some point, I put those words to the test in my own life. I found that they have truth to them. It's my observation that the greatest people I know have a strong prayer life. They have a consistent and intimate prayer life.

I often use the illustration of a table lamp. You can have the most expensive and extravagant table lamp. This lamp could be brand new and have a brand new light bulb affixed to it. If you place the lamp perfectly in the room where it will accent the decorum around it yet fail to plug it in, you just have a nice lamp. In order for the lamp to function properly and have the value of it brought out, it must be plugged into a power source. Likewise attempting to fulfill your divine purpose without prayer will render you powerless and incomplete.

What use is a lamp without power? Why would you keep a lamp that does not have the ability to produce a source of light? Chances are you would not. We have the ability to be a light. Of course, I mean that figuratively. Yet, the only way you will produce the light that is inside of you and function properly is if you are connected to the POWER SOURCE.

An active and fervent prayer life is necessary to have a deeper and meaningful relationship with God. God is the

POWER SOURCE that you will need throughout your life to stay charged. Don't underestimate the power of prayer. It is so important that you have an active prayer life that 1Thesselonians 5:17 tells us to pray without ceasing. It was so critical that one of the disciples petitioned that Jesus would teach them how to pray in Luke 11.

Luke 11:1-4(kjv) And it came to pass, that, as he was praying in a certain place, when he ceased, one of his disciples said unto him, Lord, teach us to pray, as John also taught his disciples.

² And he said unto them, When ye pray, say, Our Father which art in heaven, Hallowed be thy name. Thy kingdom come. Thy will be done, as in heaven, so in earth.

³ Give us day by day our daily bread.

⁴ And forgive us our sins; for we also forgive every one that is indebted to us. And lead us not into temptation; but deliver us from evil.

Don't treat your relationship with God like he is a genie in a lamp. Don't only seek him when you want your wishes granted or after you have exhausted all other resources. Prayer is one of those things that the more you do it, the better you get at doing it. The more you do it the closer you get to God and the stronger your relationship is with Him.

There are many things I can point to in my life that happened as a result of an active prayer life. Doors have been opened, opportunities presented, danger diverted, unmerited favor and the list goes on. It is only because my wife and I pray and have faith in God, that He hears and answers us, that we have been able to make it. We have endured some struggles in our years of marriage. I am confident that we have always come out on top because we pray. We have always been able to go through the storms of life and come out looking as if we never went in. We definitely don't look like what we've been through!

There was a time where I was not working a secular job and things were getting a little challenging. Clearly we had more going out than we had coming in and if you did the math the numbers just didn't add up. Our home had gone into foreclosure and we didn't know where we were going to go or how we were going to get there.

While all of that was going on, we still had a church to Pastor. There were people still pulling and depending on us to be whom we said God called us to be. The world doesn't stop because you have a problem. You need to be connected to the problem solver. That connection is what makes the difference. That connection will keep you out of the psychiatrist office. Isaiah 26:3 tells us that God will keep us in perfect peace if we keep our minds on Him.

We put our situation in God's hands. We didn't know what He was going to do or how He was going to fix it. It would be hypocritical for us to preach God will make a way and we not trust Him to do it. To make a long story short, God worked the situation out in our favor. He put us in a new home that was twice the size of our old home with a smaller mortgage payment.

Make prayer a regular part of your day. It's good to have a regular prayer time. Some people refer to it as a daily devotion where they read or study the Bible and pray. I think that's a great way to start but don't limit your communication with God. Throughout the day keep the lines of communication open. Pray on the way to school or work. Pray during your lunch break. Some people sing in the shower. Our son Anthony is a shower prayer. He really pours out his heart to God while he's in there. He causes me to pray about the water bill. Don't look for an excuse, the perfect time or place, just pray.

Chapter 7 questions

1. How often do you pray?

_____

_____

_____

_____

_____

2. Do you pray for others?

_____

_____

_____

_____

_____

3. When you pray do you feel God hears you?

_____

_____

_____

_____

_____

4. What time will you devote to daily scripture reading and prayer?

_____

_____

_____

_____

_____

Note# 8

<u>Learn to Communicate</u>

Earlier in the book I revealed one of my father's short comings was his inability to communicate. There have been tons of studies and articles on the communication habits of men. Most of the things I have seen written on this subject suggest that we have some serious hang-ups when it comes to this matter.

Men who don't have the ability to communicate how they feel or what they are thinking are more likely to keep emotions bottled up. You know what happens when something builds up too much pressure. At some point it explodes because it can't handle the weight of the force working against it.

As children, boys are often raised with the untruth that men are not supposed to cry. This feeds the lie that you can't have emotions. You are not supposed to express how you feel. If you are hurting just buck up and take it like a man. My thought is, if Jesus wept and he was the perfect example of a man, then it is ok for you to cry too.

It is a good idea to be in touch with how you feel. Knowing how you feel and being able to communicate that to your spouse will enhance your marriage. If you are not able to communicate your goals, dreams, doubt, fears and your inner most thoughts to your spouse, either you have married the wrong person or you just shouldn't be married.

Caring for your wife and family is your primary full time job if you are married with children. They deserve to be able to have healthy dialog and communication with you. In order for your sons not to inherit the mentality that men should just make a paycheck and not be engaging in the lives of their children, you have to engage them. Sometimes the conversation doesn't have to be about anything important. Ask how they are doing and about how their day is going. Then practice active listening. A man that is able to communicate with his family is more likely to keep his family together.

Communication is not always just about what you say. Effective communication also involves your actions.

Saying I love you and not putting that love into demonstration is empty lip service. Spending money on gifts and material things without ever saying the words I love you is just a cheap convenient knock off. In order for communication to be authentic, it must involve both words and action. One is affirming the other, both expressing the same.

In business I have always appreciated a person who is able to communicate well. Whether they are my supervisor or I am supervising them, the ability to communicate on a professional level makes for a better work environment. If moving up the corporate ladder is in your sights, you will have to know how to communicate effectively.

Many of the promotions and opportunities I have been blessed with came from my ability to communicate well with others. I was the musician and director for a number of high school gospel choirs in my city. I recall one of my students asking me what college I graduated from. When I told her I had just graduated from high school the previous year and had not yet gone to college. she was floored. She said by the way I talked and carried myself she was convinced that I was much older.

There is a level of respect associated with being a good choir director. People have to be willing to follow you and you have to be able to communicate the direction you are taking them in a very short time. The relationship between the choir director and the choir member is based on trust and communication. When these two components are working well together you have the making of a great choir. If these two things are not in place and functioning, what you might end up with is a group of people making noise. The best choirs work together, have a leader that everyone follows and he or she is able to communicate the direction they want to take the group.

I have given you a couple significant examples of communication. If you are going to lead your family, be a leader in the professional world, a leader in your community or anywhere else you have to master communication. Sometimes what you don't say is just as important as what you say. Know when to offer your opinions and know when to keep them to yourself. When people get lost in communication it usually is a recipe for disaster.

You are maturing as a young man and the world needs to hear your voice. You need to know how to communicate properly. Your lifestyle should be able to communicate who and whose you are. Keep the following scriptures in mind.

Proverbs 12:18 There is one whose rash words are like sword thrusts, but the tongue of the wise brings healing.

Ephesians 4:29 Let no corrupting talk come out of your mouths, but only such as is good for building up, as fits the occasion, that it may give grace to those who hear.

Chapter 8 questions

1. Why is communication important?

_____

_____

_____

_____

_____

_____

_____

_____

2. How did your parents communicate?

_____

_____

_____

_____

_____

_____

_____

_____

3. Do you have a problem expressing how you feel?

_____

_____

_____

_____

_____

_____

4. What steps do you think you could take to better communicate with others?

_____

_____

_____

_____

_____

_____

5. Explain Ephesians 4:29 in your own words.

_____

_____

_____

_____

_____

Note #9

When All Hell Breaks Loose

The Bible teaches that men should always pray and not faint (Luke 18:1). Perhaps this is where we get the notion that if you are a man and you show emotions under pressure, you are somehow weak and not worthy of the mantle of manhood. This is the furthest thing from the truth. Yes, men should always pray, but the fainting in this scripture is talking about giving up. You can never give up. As long as there is breath in your body, you can't give up. As long as you have a pulse, you have a reason to keep pressing forward.

We all go through some trials and tribulations. Storms in our lives will come and go. The occasional bump in the road is something that is natural. Usually you have the ability to maneuver through the storms of life and find yourself on dry land. Typically, you have a strong enough skill set to manage life's trials and tribulations. When obstacles arise, normally you will rely on past experiences along with your faith and come out on top.

Being a man who embraces and practices Kingdom Principles will serve you well as you go throughout your life. In Luke 12:22-31 Jesus taught that the Kingdom should be the primary concern of life. He concluded with this statement:

But rather seek ye the Kingdom of God; and all these things shall be added unto you. (Luke 12:31)
If you seek the Kingdom first...its principles, its lifestyle, its Gospel...then all other necessary things in life will be provided. Understanding where your help comes from and knowing that the provision of God is more than enough will comfort and keep you where others have fallen apart. The key here is that your faith must be genuine. How can your faith be genuine if it has never been tested? Prepare yourself, life happens fast and you will need faith to endure.

There have been times where faith was all I had. I have resolved within myself that whatever comes, when it seems that all hell is breaking loose around me, those are prime opportunities to totally surrender to God and trust that he knows best. I didn't say I give up or even that I didn't trust Him to begin with. What I'm saying is that after I've done all that I can, I have resolved to stand and trust in the Lord. I believe there is no sense in me losing sleep and worrying myself sick. After I have prayed about the situation, I look for God to be God.

Deuteronomy 31:6The Message (MSG)

6 "Be strong. Take courage. Don't be intimidated. Don't give them a second thought because God, your God, is striding ahead of you. He's right there with you. He won't let you down; he won't leave you.

Psalm 94:14King James Version (KJV)

14 For the Lord will not cast off his people; neither will he forsake his inheritance.

I enjoy reading the Bible to get reassurance when things are looking crazy in my life. I also like accounts where you see how God did the miraculous in someone's life and I reason within myself, if He did it for them, He will do it for me. I may not have walked on water or been thrown in a fiery furnace. Perhaps I have never turned water into wine or been raised from the dead, but those life experiences that I have endured seemed every bit as comparable in those moments of my personal crisis.

As a result of attempting to be a good parent and one of our sons making poor choices, my wife and I almost lost everything. I signed for my Oldest son to get his driver's license when he turned sixteen. The deal was he would get a job and pay for his own insurance. He and his biological mother decided to do something different. He got a car and ended up in a car accident involving several other cars and, of course, he didn't have insurance! For a few weeks prior to the accident, he was hiding the car around the corner from our house in an attempt to keep me from finding out about it. We were sued by the parties involved because I was the "Great Dad"! We had to file for bankruptcy which snow balled into greater issues.

Ultimately, we ended up losing our home which we had lived in for 12 years. Not knowing what we were going to do and simultaneously becoming unemployed from my fulltime job, we set out looking for a place to live. Every number we called, every house we looked at, turned into a dead end. We really didn't have any money, just faith. We would minister to our congregation week after week and most of them had no clue what we were dealing with in our personal life.

My simple prayer when I would talk to God was "Lord…How are you gonna fix this? You know we have to live somewhere…What are you going to do?" Within days of the auctioning of our home someone unexpectedly sowed $12,000 into our lives. As if that were not amazing enough, the next day someone else gave us their home and told us to keep all of the furniture and appliances! The house we moved into on the first Saturday in December of 2012 was at least twice as big as our former house. It was a newer home, only 10 years old and only had one owner. We walked in the front door to find they decorated the living room for Christmas along with a banner over the fireplace that said "Welcome Home Moore Family".

At the end of 2013, and for the following ten months, I cried more than any other time in my entire life. My wife had gone to work that December morning. It was right before the Christmas break. I received a phone call. The call came from my wife's cell phone but when I answered it, there was an unfamiliar woman's voice on the other end screaming that my wife had been in a terrible accident and I needed to hurry and get there.

When I arrived on the scene, her car was totaled and the fire department was putting out the fire of the other car involved in the collision. I could hear her cries as I ran to the ambulance they were putting her in. I had never heard her cry out in so much pain and it hurt me emotionally to hear her and not be able to make the pain stop for her. I had to keep it together. I had to wear the cape and be her strength. I held her hand and talked to her while they were preparing to take her to the hospital.

Although her leg was shattered on impact, witnesses talked about how she jumped out of the car when she saw the flames. She fell to the ground not realizing how bad she was hurt. Being the super woman she is, she hopped up on one leg because she had to get our God-daughter out of the back seat and to safety. Fortunately, the baby was safely fastened in her car seat.

After having surgery on her leg, my wife spent the next several weeks in a rehabilitation hospital. When she got home, we had to make trips to outpatient therapy for months. Learning to walk again wasn't easy, but she did it, one step at a time. The outpour of love and support from our family and the faith community was amazing!

Around the end of summer, when we were just getting back to normal, our son Anthony had a medical procedure done on his wrist that was supposed to be an in and out procedure. The aftermath of that procedure kept him in the hospital for ten days. After ten days of watching my son scream in pain, being dropped by hospital staff, watching him be combative and at times delusional. Having him become addicted to pain medication, being told he could die, holding him like he was a baby to comfort him even though he was a full grown man. It was as if all hell was breaking loose.

I was reminded of hearing Bishop J.D. Ellis talk about his battles with cancer. I remember him saying how it didn't matter how much of a spiritual giant you think you are; you can be in such pain that you forget to pray. Truly Anthony, who has a fervent prayer life, was in excruciating pain. During the whole ordeal, he didn't pray. My wife and I had become so distracted with doctors, nurses, administrators, concerned family and our own emotional roller coaster that we weren't warring in the spirit like we do for everyone else. I think we had a moment where we both felt helpless.

Bishop Ellis came to see Anthony in the hospital and spoke life. He could have sent someone, but he said he wanted to see Anthony for himself. When he saw him and after he prayed for him, he said 'now I know he will be alright'. It was enough for us to regain our focus. We knew that James 5:16 tells us that the prayers of the righteous avails much, however we had become distracted by the circumstance and lost sight of the solution. Intercessors had been praying, but it was time for us to trust God for our son's healing.

Take the limits off of what you think God can and will do. Your current condition isn't too hard for Him to handle. Your immediate situation isn't so massive that the Master can't manage it. When all hell is breaking loose in your life, learn to activate your faith and believe God to be God. Be willing to tell Him just where you are and what you need from him. Be grounded enough in your relationship with Him to trust that he can… But if he doesn't, he is still God!

Chapter 9 questions

1. What scripture helps you focus on God in times of crisis?

   _____

   _____

   _____

   _____

   _____

   _____

2. Identify who makes up your support system.

   _____

   _____

   _____

   _____

   _____

   _____

   _____

   _____

3. What personal situation have you endured that has strengthened your faith?

_____

_____

_____

_____

_____

_____

_____

_____

_____

_____

Note#10

It's a Small World After All

The older I get, the more I see how connected we are. It is easy to get caught up in the hustle and bustle of life. We don't plan it, but I think many people get so wrapped up in living that we forget to live. We forget that there are people around us and how significant we all are. We take too lightly the fragility of life itself; the fact that we need each other to survive.

Because of everything I hope I have instilled in you, there is a huge responsibility on your part to pull your weight. You have the ability and the tools to make a difference in the world. You can make a huge impact one day at a time, one person at a time, one situation and one choice at a time.

Every time I turn on the news or read the paper, it seems as if humanity is at war with itself. The majority of what is being reported today is about wars and rumors of wars. Everything from local violent crimes to international genocide. We have even designed new strategies to hurt each other and given them glamorous names like something out of a science fiction movie. Military Drone attacks and Cyber Warfare were never heard of twenty years ago. Now we have the technology to destroy life from the comfort of an office space and a keyboard.

Indeed, something has gone wrong with our humanity. I'm not sure if we will ever get it back, but if there is a chance for redemption it must start with our understanding of just how small the world is after all. The word of God tells us in Colossians 1:16 that "For by Him all things were created, in heaven and on earth, visible and invisible, whether thrones or dominions or rulers or authorities-all things created through him and for him".

Knowing that our origin comes from the same breath gives us a divine connection. We may not all agree on everything. We may have different ideologies and beliefs. We may have different shades of skin color. Our languages, accents, and cultural backgrounds may vary, but because we were created by God for God, it only makes sense that we honor and respect that which God created for himself.

You never know who knows who. It is essential that you treat people in the same fashion that you would want to be treated. Not only because you may need that person or someone they are connected to later on in life, but because it's the right thing to do.

I have been in positions of influence where a person was offered employment or a promotion based on my recommendation. I recently took a class where I was the oldest student in the room. Many of the other students were half my age. One young man in the class was very immature and in my opinion not a good fit for the class. I engaged him in conversation because I could see he actually had potential but lacked discipline.

At times this young man had been silly, obnoxious and borderline disrespectful. He had not been taught the relevance of always putting your best foot forward. He had noticeably become a distraction and had come very close to being removed from the class. He had no idea how my opinion and leadership in the class would weigh heavily on his completion of the course.

By the time our ten-week class was over, the young man had obviously taken some of what I shared with him to heart. I think he also understood that from my life experience and information I shared in the class, I may be someone he might need or see later on in his life. Toward the end of the class, he asked me if I would employ him or make a positive recommendation for him if I were given the opportunity. My response was, "Absolutely not!" I explained to him my answer was based on the behaviors he had displayed during our time together. There is no way, in good conscious, I could offer any positive affirmation relative to his character.

Although I believe and my prayer is that at some point he will have an awakening, that is not who he was when we met. There is an old saying that says the first impression is a lasting impression. How many first impressions have you made that have come back to haunt you? How many first impressions are you still dodging, avoiding or trying to play down long after the interaction was made? Learn to practice humility. You don't always have to be heard to be seen.

The world of technology has made the world even smaller. With the scroll of a screen or push of a button, we have the ability to directly interact with people almost anywhere in the world. Be responsible and intelligent when you post, text, email or use any other types of media. I won't go into the numerous accounts of major corporations, politicians, wealthy or prominent people who have ruined their lives and careers behind foolish and reckless things they have put on the internet.   You are smarter than that.

Your ability to make constructive associations with people will serve you well throughout your life. Being in a position to help others as well as having the type of personality that will drive people to want to help you is priceless. Remember someone is always watching. Someone is always talking. Someone is always asking about you. Always give them something good to say or give them nothing at all.

Chapter 10 questions

1. How do you personally try to make a good impression when you meet people for the first time?

_____

_____

_____

_____

_____

2. What have you done to make a positive impact on humanity?

_____

_____

_____

_____

_____

3. Give an example of how a first impression went wrong for you.

_____

_____

_____

_____

_____

_____

_____

4. Where you able to recover?

_____

_____

_____

_____

_____

_____

_____

_____

Note#11

Deal With Your Secret Sin

The Apostle Paul wrote in the book of Romans 7:15 "I did not understand what I do. For what I want to do I do not do but what I hate I do." Although Paul was a giant in the Christian faith, it is obvious here that he was conflicted. Many great leaders have fallen. Many great men have been destroyed because they refuse to deal with the conflict. They refused to confront the secret sin.

Although it was not disclosed in the letter, at least Paul was brave enough to acknowledge that he had an issue. Many men go through life putting on the facade that they have it all together. No matter how you dress "It" up, spray cologne or drape "It" in jewelry, the issue is still there. Even on our best day, we are no more than filthy rags. Our attempts to mask sin will not cover up the stench that it carries.

What is it about sin that will draw a man to his own demise? What is it about sin that drives us down a closed road and off a cliff? You may be a spiritual giant but it's that secret sin that will suddenly dwarf you if you're not willing to deal with the issue… and guess what, IT=YOU.

Perhaps you have heard that sin will take you farther than you're willing to go and keep you longer than you want to stay. Yet we embark on this journey with sin and travel down roads that were not intended for us. One of the biggest areas that men struggle with relative to this subject is sexual morality. In writing this chapter I decided to interview a varied age demographic of men. All of the men I spoke with admitted that pornography and masturbation played some role in their childhood and in many cases has carried over into their adulthood. They all agreed that it is something that is rarely openly talked about with any seriousness or resolution. For some of the men it only became a problem when their spouse discovered they still engaged in it. Other men decided to refrain from it because they felt guilty. I guess the real question is why do you masturbate? Is there something void inside of you which causes you to do it? Is there anything wrong with it at all? I am going to attempt to shed a little light on this particular subject with the hope that it will spur further dialog. This is not a simple subject but remember it is always good to practice self-control.

Personally I find myself torn between the following three opinions.

1.   The Professional: While managing a sex offender unit in a juvenile facility, the therapist on our staff counseled the young men in my care to practice masturbation in private as one of the alternatives to sexually offending. While you may find professionals having varied clinical opinions on this practice, it makes sense to me from the position that it is a better option than committing a sexual crime. Masturbation in privacy is not illegal but remember it is always better to practice self-control.

2.   The Pastor: From a spiritual leader's point of view I will always teach from the pulpit from the perspective that we are not our own and that we should honor God with our bodies. Practicing self-control is honorable. I have counseled people who are addicted to pornography. It consumes them, causing issues in their marriages and other relationships. Indeed, sex outside of the marital union is

not something a Christian should engage in. God created sex to be pleasurable and enjoyed by a man and a woman who are united together in a marital covenant. Yet there are no specific instructions relative to masturbation. The very things that are often shunned or considered too risky for church conversation must be talked about in the church. We need to talk about masturbation and pornography and not just from the perspective of DON'T DO IT. Remember, it is always better to practice self-control.

3.   The Parent: As a father I teach my sons that you need to wait to have sex with your wife. I would hope that you have prayerfully sought out the woman that God has shaped for you. However, I refuse to be so heavenly bound that I'm not living in my earthly reality. I can't be with my sons 24 hours seven days a week until they get married. The fact is that young ladies are just as curious about sex as young men, both with hormones raging out of control. I have seen people with strong faith convictions be weakened under the right conditions. As a father I want my sons to abstain, but I would be irresponsible if I didn't have a conversation with them about condoms and

protecting themselves from unplanned pregnancy and disease. Included in that conversation we must talk about masturbation from a spiritual, moral and health perspective. Remember it is always better to practice self-control.

I am sure you noticed the extra emphasis I have put on self-control. The American Psychological Association defines willpower (self-control) as; the ability to delay gratification, resisting short-term temptations in order to meet long-term goals. Perhaps it won't be that first drink or that first hit from smoking marijuana. Maybe you don't realize how much you enjoy pornography and masturbation until you realize how in the middle of the night it regularly drives you to a dark room in your house; with only the glare of a computer monitor illuminating the room and the dark corners of your mind. Hours pass until the glare from the screen is diminished by the sunrise of a new morning and you realized you've done it again.

One of the men I interviewed shared with me a story that was told to him at a Christian retreat. He said that everything has its place and the place God intended for a man's semen is to his wife. Consider this, if you have to keep it a secret it probably isn't worth engaging in. Cheating on your wife, drug and alcohol addictions, white collar crime, cheating on your taxes. If it does not honor God, if it brings shame to you or your family, chances are you should refrain from doing it.

Because we are all individually made, what may entice me may not entice you. What may consume you may not move me at all. But remember our adversary is subtle and cunning. Don't allow what may seem like a simple meaningless act snowball into something that opens up a gateway to bondage. Don't allow a fleeting moment and your lack of self-control to stifle your future and long-term goal.

The Bible teaches us that whom the son sets free is free indeed. The choice to be free is totally up to you. The moment you decide to walk in that type of freedom may cause you to lose significant relationships. After all, misery loves company and there will be those who will try to keep you bound. We must learn to be doers of the word and learn how to flee from the very appearance of sin. If our adversary is able to keep his hand on us, he is able to keep us in bondage. If we are kept in bondage, we lose our ability to walk in the liberty that is associated with Calvary and Christ's victory. Don't walk the tightrope of sin, it only leads to destruction.

Samson thought he had mastered the tightrope act when he was able to keep the secret of his strength from Delilah. It was that last attempt that finally exhausted Samson and caused him to give in to her enticements. The enemy will be subtle yet relentless in his attempts to trap you. You must be alert and prayed up. It is not a matter of if you will be tempted and tried, it's a matter of when is the test coming and are you prepared?

It's always sad to watch your heroes fall because they didn't deal with the "issue". What should have been dealt with and avoided is ultimately minimized and protected. Once the "issue" is not confronted, it is given permission to take root and grow. You have to kill it before it kills you.

The Bible says in Proverbs 28:13 "He who conceals his transgressions will not prosper, but he who confesses and forsakes them will find compassion." I know you are probably thinking that there are plenty of people who try to conceal their sins that seem to be prospering. The real question is, are they prospering or do they merely exist? Sure some may have more money, more friends or more materialistic things than you, but I would rather have peace of mind and God's compassion.

Secret sins will have you ducking and dodging, always worried about who may find out. If they find out, what will they think of me? Secret sins carry a burden and stress with them that will, at some point, take its toll on you. Avoid it like the plague. Expose it and run the other way. James 4:7 tells us if we resist the devil he will flee from you. It's hard to resist something that you have allowed unlimited access. That is why it is important that you confront it when it comes for you. Confront it, overcome it and reap the benefits of living bondage free.

Samson found himself in a place where he was captured, tortured and made into an object of sport. His eyes were plucked out and he was paraded around and ridiculed all because he didn't deal with his "issue".

Surely this wise man did not foresee the condition he found himself in. Fortunately, he came to his senses long enough to repent and ask God for his strength back in order to destroy those who had captured him.

If you find yourself entangled and trapped, remember God is there waiting for you to repent. God wants to show his compassion on you. God wants to restore you, but you have to be strong enough to turn to him and receive His compassion. The easiest way to keep from getting consumed by secret sin is to stop it before it starts.

Chapter 11 questions

1.   What are some potential repercussions of secret sin?

_____

_____

_____

_____

_____

_____

2.   Has secret sin ever played a role in your life? How did you get free?

_____

_____

_____

_____

_____

_____

3.   What issues did Samson have?

_____

_____

_____

_____

_____

_____

_____

4.   Do you have someone who you are accountable to
     and can be transparent with? If not why?

_____

_____

_____

_____

_____

_____

_____

Now that you have come to the end of this book, I hope you will implement some, if not all of these notes in your life. I hope you were honest with yourself in answering the questions at the end of each note and that it causes you to reflect on a deeper level. There are many more lessons in life to be learned. Hopefully these notes will serve as a road map or point of reference along your journey.

When you were a child, you spoke as a child, understood as a child and naturally did the things children do. Perhaps it is time to rise to the call of the man inside of you. While you cannot change or undo the past, you have the ability to shape your future. What will you do? What changes will you be brave enough to make toward being the best man that you can be? The possibilities for your bright future are endless and the choice is all yours.

www.ingramcontent.com/pod-product-compliance
Lightning Source LLC
Chambersburg PA
CBHW060948040426
42445CB00011B/1059